Bible reflections
for older people

BRF

The Bible Reading Fellowship
15 The Chambers, Vineyard
Abingdon OX14 3FE
brf.org.uk

The Bible Reading Fellowship (BRF) is a Registered Charity (233280)

ISBN 978 0 85746 774 4

Acknowledgements
Scripture quotations marked NIV taken from The Holy Bible, New International Version (Anglicised edition) copyright © 1979, 1984, 2011 by Biblica. Used by permission of Hodder & Stoughton Publishers, a Hachette UK company. All rights reserved. 'NIV' is a registered trademark of Biblica. UK trademark number 1448790.

Scripture quotations marked NRSV from The New Revised Standard Version of the Bible, Anglicised edition, copyright © 1989, 1995 by the Division of Christian Education of the National Council of the Churches of Christ in the United States of America. Used by permission. All rights reserved.

Scripture quotations marked GNB from the Good News Bible published by The Bible Societies/HarperCollins Publishers Ltd, UK © American Bible Society 1966, 1971, 1976, 1992, used with permission.

Scripture quotations marked RSV from The Revised Standard Version of the Bible, copyright © 1946, 1952, 1971 by the Division of Christian Education of the National Council of the Churches of Christ in the United States of America. Used by permission. All rights reserved.

Scripture quotations marked NKJV taken from the New King James Version®. Copyright © 1982 by Thomas Nelson. Used by permission. All rights reserved.

'Sunrise, on May Morning' on page 34 © Robert Ferguson. From Late Starter (AuthorHouse UK, 2018). Used with kind permission.

Every effort has been made to trace and contact copyright owners for material used in this resource. We apologise for any inadvertent omissions or errors, and would ask those concerned to contact us so that full acknowledgement can be made in the future.

A catalogue record for this book is available from the British Library

Printed and bound in the UK by Zenith Media NP4 0DQ

Contents

About the writers

Erica Roberts is a former paediatric oncologist and palliative care specialist. As an Anglican priest, she is passionate about her growing role as a City Chaplain for Older People in Southampton and as part of The Gift of Years network. She is a regular contributor on BBC Radio Solent and loves being creative in worship and engaging those who live with dementia.

David Winter is a former producer and Head of Religious Broadcasting at the BBC. He is also the author of 43 books, the most recent being *Heaven's Morning: Rethinking the destination* (BRF, 2016). Now retired from full-time ministry, he lives in Berkshire.

Anne Townsend is a former OMF missionary doctor in Thailand. She has written a number of books including *Faith without Pretending* (Hodder, 1990) and was the founding editor of *Christian Family* magazine. She is a psychotherapist and a (supposedly) retired priest in the Church of England. She is also the granny of six, mother of three and wife of one.

David Butterfield was successful in the 2017 writing competition for readers of *The Upper Room* Bible reading notes. After studying music, he felt the call to ordination in the Church of England. During his 40-year ministry, he served at churches in Southport, the Midlands and Shropshire. His final post was based at York Minster, from which he retired in 2017. He and his wife Irene now live in Ripon in North Yorkshire. They have two adult children.

From the Editor

Welcome to this new collection of Bible reflections.

I wasn't sure about the BBC programme, *The Real Marigold Hotel*. Based on two successful British films of similar titles, the idea was to take a group of older British celebrities to try out retirement in India.

I didn't watch at first but, channel-hopping one evening, I caught an episode from series three and was captivated. Unlike most 'reality TV', it didn't focus on people falling out and moaning behind each other's backs. No one seriously believed that this eclectic cast might actually retire to India, but the possibility was intriguing. The celebrities' month-long stay in a charming old Haveli in the Lake City of Udaipur led to some revealing reflections about ageing and identity, not least from former television presenter Selina Scott:

'I don't see myself as old,' she said, 'I mean, it is silly, because I know I'm old. But when we talk about retirement, it's like talking about someone else.'

'Who are we as we get older?' is the question Erica Roberts explores, with warmth and wisdom, in the first series of reflections in this issue and, in different ways, the other writers all touch on the same theme.

I hope you enjoy all our writers' contributions and find insight, encouragement and inspiration in their words.

God bless you

Using these reflections

Perhaps you have always had a special daily time for reading the Bible and praying. But now, as you grow older, you are finding it more difficult to keep to a regular pattern or find it hard to concentrate. Or maybe you've never done this before. Whatever your situation, these Bible reflections aim to help you take a few moments to read God's word and pray, whenever you have time or feel that would be helpful.

When to read them

You may find it helpful to use these Bible reflections in the morning or last thing at night, or any time during the day. There are 40 daily reflections here, grouped around four themes. Each one includes some verses from the Bible, a reflection to help you in your own thinking about God, and a prayer suggestion. The reflections aren't dated, so it doesn't matter if you don't want to read every day. The Bible verses are printed, but if you'd like to read from your own Bible that's fine too.

How to read them

- **Take time** to quieten yourself, becoming aware of God's presence, asking him to speak to you through the Bible and the reflection.

- **Read** the Bible verses and the reflection:
  - What do you especially like or find helpful in these verses?
  - What might God be saying to you through this reading?
  - Is there something to pray about or thank God for?

- **Pray.** Each reflection includes a prayer suggestion. You might like to pray for yourself or take the opportunity to think about and pray for others.

Who am I?

Erica Roberts

See what great love the Father has lavished on us, that we should be called children of God!

1 JOHN 3:1 (NIV)

Socrates, the Greek philosopher, famously said, 'Man, know thyself. The unexamined life is not worth living.'

Who am I? Exploring this fundamental question about our identity and our unique place in the world is exciting, but it can also be perplexing as we weave together the different strands that make us so wonderfully individual.

Unfortunately, we are often tempted to define ourselves by what we do, what we have or what other people think of us. As we enter our later years, reflecting on our identity is further challenged as we inevitably change roles, whether through retirement or in our community, in the church or at home.

Rooted in his own relationship with the Father, Jesus shows us that our deepest identity can be discovered as a child of God. This profound truth is reflected through the prism of the great love that God lavishes on each of us, a truth that reminds us of our eternal value to God, whoever we are, whatever we do and however the world views us – a truth we will explore together in these reflections.

Ephesians 2:10 (NIV)

I am God's work of art

For we are God's handiwork, created in Christ Jesus to do good works, which God prepared in advance for us to do.

Discovering a small art gallery, with its hidden treasures, is always a delight, and I'm continually surprised and moved by the creativity depicted through pen, paint and all manner of unusual objects. However, the piece of art that has had the most profound impact on me – that has stirred my heart and soul – is the tragic beauty conveyed by Michelangelo's *Pietà*, a sculpture of Mary tenderly holding Jesus after his death.

There is a story once told in which Michelangelo, studying a large, untouched block of marble and assessing the potential hidden within, declared that he could see an angel imprisoned in the marble, and that it must be set free. He believed that the artist had access to the soul image within the marble block.

Similarly, God sees our image on his heart before we are formed, and, as Paul describes so beautifully, we are created in the image of Jesus; God has crafted an eternal and unique identity for each of us. This process may sometimes be painful, as God, the master sculptor, chips away at the unwanted marble, but eventually we will all be shaped into God's beautiful masterpiece.

■ **PRAYER**

Creator God, thank you for forming me in the image of Jesus Christ. Help me to reflect his beauty to those around me today. Amen

Isaiah 43:1b (NIV)

I am called by name

'Do not fear, for I have redeemed you; I have summoned you by name; you are mine.'

Names matter. Whether we like our own name or not, names identify us; they are bound up in our history and our understanding of each other. Walking on the moors, I love identifying myself with the purple hue of the heather: wild, adventurous and beautiful. Erica (my name!) is the botanical name for this shrub, and Heather just happens to be my mother's name.

Most importantly, our names matter because they reflect an intimacy and a deep connection with those who call us by name. Being named by God speaks of the intimate relationship he desires to have with each of us. God calls us to be in his presence, to belong to him and to be protected by him through all the trials that life may bring.

This promise of intimacy, love and protection is conveyed by the wonderful image of being bound eternally to God, when he declares, 'I will not forget you! See, I have engraved you on the palms of my hands' (Isaiah 49:15–16). Whatever the experience we've had of our own name, today let's be confident that we are so precious to God that he continues to call us into an intimate and loving relationship with himself.

■ **PRAYER**

Heavenly Father, thank you for calling me by name. Help me to draw even closer to you. Amen

1 Samuel 16:1 (NIV, abridged)

I am chosen

The Lord said to Samuel… 'Fill your horn with oil and be on your way; I am sending you to Jesse of Bethlehem. I have chosen one of his sons to be king.'

Most of us will know the story of David, the young herdsman, tending his sheep. This youngest son of Jesse was chosen over his older, more qualified brothers to be anointed as king of Israel. Choosing David for this role couldn't have been more unexpected, but, as God explained, 'The Lord does not look at the things people look at. People look at the outward appearance, but the Lord looks at the heart' (1 Samuel 16:7).

Of course, David wasn't perfect – far from it – but he remained faithful to God throughout his successes, failures and struggles, as illustrated so vividly in some of his psalms. I wonder if you have ever been chosen for an unexpected role and then discovered how God can equip you despite your deepest misgivings. God knows our hearts, and only God sees the wider context in which we are chosen to serve, a truth that continues throughout our lives.

In our older years, we can trust God to choose us to serve him with our unique experiences and gifts, as we discover God's continuing purpose for us in this season of our lives.

■ **PRAYER**

Lord Jesus, you chose me for a purpose: to abide in your love and to bear fruit. Help me to discern your chosen role for me today. Amen

Luke 12:6–7 (NIV)

I am significant

'Are not five sparrows sold for two pennies? Yet not one of them is forgotten by God. Indeed, the very hairs of your head are all numbered. Don't be afraid; you are worth more than many sparrows.'

Growing older can be a great joy as we discover the gift of time to explore new interests, to relish family and friends and to deepen our relationship with God. But it is not like this all the time. Who are we when we retire, when our children become independent, when we lose someone we love or when we hand the baton of responsibility on to the younger generation?

Confronted by a world that defines success as significance, there is a challenge for us in later life to re-examine our purpose and meaning. Our significance can only truly be understood through the knowledge of our value to our creator God, gloriously made in his image and known intimately by him. Not only does God know each hair on our head, but, in old age and grey hairs, God promises to sustain us (Isaiah 46:4).

C.S. Lewis, in *The Weight of Glory* (1949), declares, 'There are no ordinary people. You have never met a mere mortal.' What a wonderful reflection that God sees us all as extraordinary. Knowing our significance before God, how can we begin to affirm the worth of those around us, whatever their age?

■ **PRAYER**

We praise you, Father, for the wonderful truth that everyone is significant to you. Help me to value others through your eyes. Amen

1 John 4:7, 19 (NIV)

I am loved

Dear friends, let us love one another, for love comes from God. Everyone who loves has been born of God and knows God... We love because he first loved us.

These two verses act as bookends to this revealing passage about God's incredible love for us. Not only is it clear that being loved by God is the very essence of our identity, but this love that has formed us and informs us demands a response of love from us. Medical research demonstrates that being loved contributes positively to our health and well-being and improves our lifespan.

Discovering our identity through being loved is beautifully illustrated in the much-loved children's book, *The Velveteen Rabbit* by Margery Williams (1922). In the book, the Skin Horse explains to the Rabbit how to become real: 'Real is a thing that happens to you. When a child loves you for a long, long time, not just to play with, but REALLY loves you, then you become Real.'

In God's love for us, we too become real, growing into our full potential. Held securely in that love, the only response is to love God and to learn to love others, not just our friends but also those we find hard to love. Spend some time now basking in that truth: 'We love because he first loved us.' I wonder who God is calling us to love today?

■ PRAYER

Loving God, help me to love others as I grow in your love for me. Amen

1 Corinthians 12:26b–27 (NIV)

Part of the body

If one part is honoured, every part rejoices with it. Now you are the body of Christ, and each one of you is a part of it.

I love nothing better than gathering a group of friends around my kitchen table; it doesn't matter what meal we're sharing, but drawing people together, listening to each other's stories, laughing and sometimes shedding tears reminds me that it is through this sense of belonging that I discover more of my own identity.

We are made to be in relationship with each other and to share our common, broken humanity. Jean Vanier, founder of the L'Arche communities (a worldwide network of communities for those who are cognitively impaired and their caregivers), believes that 'we do not discover who we are, we do not reach true humanness, in a solitary state; we discover it through mutual dependency, in weakness, in learning through belonging'.*

In this passage to the church in Corinth, Paul is reminding us that the human body only functions effectively when each unique part is fulfilling its specific role. We all have an equally important part to play in ensuring that our community works together for the glory of God; this is true for all of us, including the most vulnerable and frail. The body of Christ is stronger when we seek to embrace those who are struggling and those who are most dependent.

■ **PRAYER**

Lord Jesus, as part of your body, help me to honour others, so we can live together in peace and unity. Amen

*Jean Vanier, *Becoming Human* (Darton, Longman and Todd, 1999).

1 John 5:14 (NIV)

I am heard

This is the confidence we have in approaching God: that if we ask anything according to his will, he hears us.

To be in the presence of someone who listens well is affirming and helps us to feel valued for who we are. In a society with ever-advancing technology, it's challenging to listen attentively. Unfortunately, the advent of the mobile phone has been a huge distraction for me. However, I love the immediacy of contacts from far and wide and access to world events in real time, so, with difficulty, I'm still learning how to overcome the temptation of having it constantly at my side.

I wonder what distracts you from listening well. Even when we're a good listener, it's not easy to be attentive if we're bored, tired or preoccupied with our own situation. To be heard is a gift, and yet we're not always aware of the difference between waiting to speak and intentionally listening.

Wonderfully, we have a God who always hears us, who is interested in the smallest detail of our lives and who hears our call – 'The Lord hears when I call to him' (Psalm 4:3) – and the sound of our tears – 'The Lord has heard my weeping' (Psalm 6:8). No distractions, no mobiles: God is present with us, listening, hearing and always answering. But are we listening for his voice in return?

■ PRAYER
Gracious God, help me to listen attentively to both you and the world around me. Amen

Psalm 139:1 (NIV)

I am known

You have searched me, Lord, and you know me.

Our deepest identity is profoundly expressed in the truth that God knows us intimately. As the psalmist continues, there is nothing about us that isn't familiar to God and there is nowhere we can go to flee from God's knowledge of us. As we read earlier, Jesus says to his disciples that even 'the very hairs of your head are all numbered. Don't be afraid; you are worth more than many sparrows' (Luke 12:7) – and not one sparrow is forgotten by God.

What a wonderful expression of God's unconditional love: we are not only intimately known and valuable to him, but also never forgotten by him. Being known means that we are also remembered and, recognising the struggle of friends living with dementia, this promise from God is deeply affirming.

John Swinton, a practical theologian, writes, 'To be remembered by God is to endure in the present and into eternity – our identity is safe in the memory of God.'* Whoever we are, including those whose memory is failing, we are all known and remembered by God. Not only are we all held in this moment by God's knowledge and love, but we are all called to remind others, especially those who do not remember, that they too are known and loved by God.

■ **PRAYER**

Lord Jesus, let me rest in this moment, confident that I am known and loved by you. Amen

*John Swinton, *Dementia: Living in the memories of God* (SCM Press, 2012).

Micah 7:19 (NIV)

I am forgiven

You will again have compassion on us; you will tread our sins underfoot and hurl all our iniquities into the depths of the sea.

God understands that our past mistakes can lead to wounds that we carry for years, marring our sense of identity. Left untouched, these wounds can fester, leading to guilt and pain that prevent us from living in the freedom that God has promised.

I wonder if you have ever skimmed stones on the edge of the sea? I love the idea that those stones represent our sin and regrets. We watch them skim towards the horizon and then disappear, sinking deep into the ocean.

Corrie ten Boom, imprisoned in Ravensbrück for harbouring Jews, understood both the importance and the challenge of forgiveness. Corrie explained, 'When we confess our sins, God casts them into the deepest ocean, gone forever. And, even though I cannot find a scripture for it, I believe God then places a sign out there that says, "NO FISHING ALLOWED".'*

Knowing that we are forgiven is fundamental to our Christian faith and identity. The sacrifice made by Jesus for us on the cross means that we are forgiven – and no fishing is allowed. Are we prepared to let go of our stones today and accept that forgiveness offered by Jesus?

■ PRAYER

God of mercy, help us to know that our sins are forgiven and forgotten. Amen

*Corrie ten Boom, Tramp for the Lord (1971).

Luke 14:16–17 (NIV)

I am invited

Jesus replied: 'A certain man was preparing a great banquet and invited many guests. At the time of the banquet he sent his servant to tell those who had been invited, "Come, for everything is now ready."'

I love a good party. I enjoy planning and preparing for the festivities, from children's themed parties to celebrations for anniversaries and life events. We have recently given thanks in church for a lovely couple's 65th wedding anniversary; we heard their story, prayed for them and then shared cake. What makes a party special, of course, is being surrounded by our family and friends and sharing the celebration with those who are most significant in our lives.

In today's scripture, Jesus teaches about the kingdom of God through the parable of the great banquet, a parable which illustrates that everyone is invited to God's party and that no one is excluded. Jesus throws parties for the outcast, the homeless, the misfit – not just those who are popular or who make the party swing. Jesus invites those who feel unworthy and unloved and seats them in the place of honour. In God's kingdom, each of us is equally valued and loved.

What amazingly good news! We are all invited to a party that transcends our earthly life, and God says there is still more room at the table. I wonder who we know who would like an invitation?

■ **PRAYER**

Lord Jesus, show me today who to invite to your party. Amen

Timothy, my child

David Winter

It's something most of us have experienced as we've grown older: there was a time when we helped and guided a younger person and then, as the years wore on, we found the roles gently reversed.

In these reflections, we'll be reading from the apostle Paul's second letter to Timothy, the young man whom he first met at Lystra, and then took with him on his second missionary journey. Clearly impressed, Paul began to give Timothy more and more responsibility, sending him to Thessalonica and Corinth, and then giving him a leadership role at Ephesus. This second letter of Paul's, full of affection and warmth, shows how close the older and the younger man were, but it also reveals how their relationship was slowly changing.

The letter itself is rather odd: a strange mix of deeply personal, intimate messages alongside passages of doctrine and exhortation. The intimate messages from the great apostle to the man he called 'my child' give a unique and touching insight into the very heart of Paul as he prepared for what he already knew lay ahead. He was martyred in Rome in 65AD.

I hope that, as we look at these honest and revealing little glimpses into a relationship that bridged the generations, we may see how, over our lifetime, God uses our human commitments and caring both to bless us and make us a blessing. Step forward, Paul, and your 'beloved child' Timothy.

2 Timothy 1:1–3 (NRSV)

My beloved child

Paul, an apostle of Christ Jesus by the will of God, for the sake of the promise of life that is in Christ Jesus, To Timothy, my beloved child: Grace, mercy, and peace from God the Father and Christ Jesus our Lord. I am grateful to God – whom I worship with a clear conscience, as my ancestors did – when I remember you constantly in my prayers night and day.

This is a typical formal opening to a letter from Paul. He is writing as an 'apostle', a position of great authority in the early church. He was appointed by God, no less, and he is writing to Timothy, whom he describes as his 'beloved child', even though Timothy was probably over 30 years old at this time. Paul had no children of his own: why, then, this very intimate title?

Paul had met Timothy's family around twelve years earlier, when he came to Ephesus on his first missionary journey. It was a family with a problem: it had a Jewish Christian mother and a Gentile unbeliever father. But Paul clearly recognised some spiritual potential in Timothy and circumcised the young man, thus confirming his Jewish roots.

Paul came to regard Timothy as his trusted assistant, and his letter finds Timothy in Ephesus, carrying out pastoral duties. Both of his letters to Timothy are full of instructions: do this, avoid doing this. But through them all, there is also a growing note of trust and affection.

■ PRAYER

Loving God, there is someone who needs my prayers 'night and day'. Help me to be faithful and constant in prayer. Amen

2 Timothy 1:4–5 (NRSV)

Tears and joy

Recalling your tears, I long to see you so that I may be filled with joy. I am reminded of your sincere faith, a faith that lived first in your grandmother Lois and your mother Eunice and now, I am sure, lives in you.

This is quite a change of mood from the formal initial greeting. What is the cause of these 'tears'? Were they shed when Timothy left for Ephesus, sent there by Paul? With the apostle's life threatened by the Roman authorities, these two men might never meet on earth again. Whatever the reasons, the tears speak of a closeness of affection that goes beyond a working relationship or even a shared Christian commitment. Here are two men, one in his 60s, the other around 30 years younger, who have come to depend on each other.

That, I think, is relevant to most of us who are older. When we agreed 30 years ago to be a godmother to our best friend's new baby, or to pray for someone who had just become a Christian as a teenager, our relationship with them was essentially one-sided. We prayed for them, kept in touch, followed their life story. But eventually the little baby is at university, or the former teenager has serious problems at work. We still pray for them, not because we are strong and they are weak, but because of our commitment to their wholeness. Soon, we may find, it will be their turn to pray for us.

■ **PRAYER**

Lord, bless these special relationships, and keep the flame of faith alive within them. Amen

2 Timothy 1:12b–14 (NRSV)

Guarding the good treasure

But I am not ashamed, for I know the one in whom I have put my trust, and I am sure that he is able to guard until that day what I have entrusted to him. Hold to the standard of sound teaching that you have heard from me, in the faith and love that are in Christ Jesus. Guard the good treasure entrusted to you, with the help of the Holy Spirit living in us.

Several times in these epistles, there are passages that seem to be quotations, perhaps from prayers or hymns familiar in the first-century church. Sometimes the writer calls them 'faithful sayings'. This one is an assertion of faith: 'I know in whom I have put my trust.' Not only that, but the one I trust is able to 'guard' what I've entrusted to him. Faith, as the New Testament knows it, starts and ends with Jesus.

The gospel that had transformed Paul and Timothy's lives is 'good treasure', which they need to guard constantly. But here, too, help is at hand through the Holy Spirit who lives in them. These are verses of great assurance, both for those who are long-term pilgrims and for those struggling with unexpected rebuffs. 'I am sure that he is able': not that I am, nor that my young friend is, but that our Saviour is able – our guardian and our guide.

■ **PRAYER**

May we and those we pray for know in times of testing the 'faith and love that are in Christ Jesus'. Amen

2 Timothy 2:11–13 (NRSV)

He remains faithful

The saying is sure: If we have died with him, we will also live with him; if we endure, we will also reign with him; if we deny him, he will also deny us; if we are faithless, he remains faithful – for he cannot deny himself.

This is another 'faithful saying' (the literal meaning of 'the saying is sure'). Doubtless both Paul and Timothy would have known the saying and, in their present circumstances, would find strength from it. It consists of a series of contrasts, beginning with the word 'If'.

'If we have died with him' refers to baptism – 'buried with him in baptism' was Paul's phrase. But those who 'died' with Christ also 'live' with him. The word 'live' is present tense; we are alive in Christ now. Then if we stay the course – 'endure' – that living will become reigning with him: sharing in the joy of the kingdom of heaven. The next pair of contrasts is different: to 'deny' Jesus would be a terrible thing, but being 'faithless' feels like a more familiar failing.

To interpret these sayings, I like to think of two of the chosen apostles, Judas Iscariot and Thomas. Judas denied Jesus when he betrayed him, thus putting himself outside the community of Christ's disciples. Thomas, on the other hand, did not deny Jesus but he was unbelieving ('faithless') over the claims of the others to have seen the risen Jesus. For Thomas, Jesus remained faithful. Jesus trusted Thomas to realise his weakness and to learn to trust, without evidence of sight or touch.

■ **PRAYER**

Lord, help me to believe even where I cannot know, and trust where I cannot see. Amen

2 Timothy 2:20–22 (NRSV)

Beautiful utensils

In a large house there are utensils not only of gold and silver but also of wood and clay, some for special use, some for ordinary. All who cleanse themselves of the things I have mentioned will become special utensils, dedicated and useful to the owner of the house, ready for every good work. Shun youthful passions and pursue righteousness, faith, love, and peace, along with those who call on the Lord from a pure heart.

This is also surely a 'faithful saying' – or someone's notes for a sermon illustration. It isn't what we are – boring old saucepans or classical teapots – but what God makes of us that matters. He can take whatever we bring to him and transform it into a 'utensil' for his glorious purposes. Some things in the kitchen may be beautiful; others may be functional. And the same is true of the church.

I don't think what follows is personal advice for Timothy, but I do think it is wonderful day-by-day advice. The 'youthful passions' may have abated, but there are now the elderly ones – in my case, for instance, the angry frustration that I can no longer do things I once enjoyed. Turning away from the negative instincts, we can 'pursue' – I love that word – faith, love and peace to become effective utensils, and beautiful ones as well.

■ **PRAYER**

Heavenly Father, deliver me from unhelpful and negative thoughts, and help me to pursue faith, love and peace. Amen

2 Timothy 3:14–15 (NRSV)

Never too early to start

But as for you, continue in what you have learned and firmly believed, knowing from whom you learned it, and how from childhood you have known the sacred writings that are able to instruct you for salvation through faith in Christ Jesus.

'But as for you...'. Paul turns from an emotional narrative of his own ministry and suffering to offer advice to his younger colleague. He knows Timothy's family background, of course, and the faith of his grandmother and mother. He urges Timothy to continue on the path in life he had known from his childhood. The authenticity of his faith lay in its sources: 'knowing from whom you learned it'. That is a measure of the responsibility each of us bears: it was because of who they were that the words of Lois and Eunice had so deeply influenced the young Timothy.

What the child Timothy had learnt from the women in his life was the importance of the 'sacred writings' – the Hebrew scriptures that we call the Old Testament. Their promises and prophecies had led Lois and Eunice to faith in Jesus Christ, and the young boy had followed in their footsteps. His was a faith built on firm foundations, and it is a huge privilege for any of us to have such a role in someone's faith journey.

■ **PRAYER**

Thank you, Lord, for those who once showed me the way to Christ. Help me to follow their example. Amen

2 Timothy 4:1–2 (NRSV)

Urgent, but patient

In the presence of God and of Christ Jesus, who is to judge the living and the dead, and in view of his appearing and his kingdom, I solemnly urge you: proclaim the message; be persistent whether the time is favourable or unfavourable; convince, rebuke, and encourage, with the utmost patience in teaching.

Here, in two sentences, is Paul's picture of Christian ministry, which he now urges Timothy to follow. It is, to put it mildly, very demanding, and to be fulfilled under the eye of the one who will ultimately judge all of us, whether ministers or lay people.

What strikes me about this advice is its urgency. The early church expected the imminent return of Jesus, which meant that time was short. Of course, eventually Christians came to realise that the time of his coming again – in whatever form that would take – was unknown on earth (2 Peter 3:3–8). Yet the urgency remains. We are not immortal; the message of the gospel is urgent; and there is no 'favourable' or 'unfavourable' time for sharing it.

At the same time, the Christian witness must both 'rebuke' and 'encourage' with what Paul calls 'the utmost patience'. I suspect patience was a gift of the Spirit that Paul himself especially struggled to attain. That reminds us that what we have here is a picture of 'perfect' Christian ministry – and not one of us has ever experienced that.

■ **PRAYER**

Christian ministry is difficult and demanding. In prayer and encouragement, Lord, may we support those you have called to it. Amen

2 Timothy 4:6–8 (NRSV)

But as for me...

As for me, I am already being poured out as a libation, and the time of my departure has come. I have fought the good fight, I have finished the race, I have kept the faith. From now on there is reserved for me the crown of righteousness, which the Lord, the righteous judge, will give to me on that day, and not only to me but also to all who have longed for his appearing.

Paul has given his message to Timothy – 'as for you'. It's now 'as for me'. How did he stand as he contemplated a series of trials that would almost certainly end in his execution? The answer is a statement of Christian confidence – not in himself, but in the one who had called him.

A 'libation' was a precious drink poured out in worship. Paul would be that 'libation'. The fight has been fought; the race he has often spoken of is reaching the finishing line; the faith he has embraced is still secure. He looks forward to the promised rewards. The spiritual confidence he expresses is in marked contrast to the practical disappointments that the rest of the letter express, but that is not a contradiction. Often, surely, we all face the contrast between life as God intends it and the everyday setbacks of life as it is. God never said it would be easy. The crown is not for never being sad – but for never giving up the fight.

■ **PRAYER**

Lord, help me, by your grace alone, to fight the good fight, to run the race and to keep the faith. Amen

2 Timothy 4:9–13, 21a (NRSV)

A cry for help

Do your best to come to me soon, for Demas, in love with this present world, has deserted me and gone to Thessalonica; Crescens has gone to Galatia, Titus to Dalmatia. Only Luke is with me. Get Mark and bring him with you, for he is useful in my ministry. I have sent Tychicus to Ephesus. When you come, bring the cloak that I left with Carpus at Troas, also the books, and above all the parchments… Do your best to come before winter.

Paul never married and we hear nothing of his family. However, from the time of his conversion on the road to Damascus, he was never short of friends, fellow workers and companions. But now, when he needs them most, they're not there. Other interests, illness or even Christian ministry have taken them off to various places. Some have simply 'deserted' him. 'Only Luke is with me.' Only? His long-standing friend, and a doctor. That 'only' jumps off the page. When we're feeling down, we find it hard to recognise even the good things.

So the great apostle shares the kind of experience most of us have had at some time or other: 'Where are you when I need you?' Once, Timothy needed Paul's guidance and fatherly help. Now, Paul needs the younger man's support and company – and the cloak, books and parchment – before winter. I can't think of a more revealing phrase in all Paul's letters than the simple plea, 'Do your best to come before winter.' This is the cry of the heavy heart: a simple human need.

Of course, deep down, Paul still knows that he is not alone: 'But the Lord stood by me' (2 Timothy 4:17). No, never alone.

■ PRAYER

Heavenly Father, when the inevitable setbacks and disappointments come, may I know that you are with me. Amen

2 Timothy 4:19–22a (NRSV)

Brothers and sisters

Greet Prisca and Aquila, and the household of Onesiphorus. Erastus remained in Corinth; Trophimus I left ill in Miletus. Do your best to come before winter. Eubulus sends greetings to you, as do Pudens and Linus and Claudia and all the brothers and sisters. The Lord be with your spirit. Grace be with you.

Many years ago, I remember a young doctor, a Christian, telling me that he had got on a train from York to London without anything to read. He decided on an impulse to spend the journey thinking of all his Christian friends and praying for them. He had been dreading the long journey, but was moved and inspired by the experience. The journey went so quickly!

When I am tempted to skip passages like this one, which could be seen simply as personal messages to people we don't know, I remember that doctor. He did what Paul does here: tapped into the rich blessing of the 'communion of saints', the 'brothers and sisters' God has given us for love and support. As we saw in the previous passage, some people may let us down, but there are a host of others on our side. And among them, above all others for Paul, is Timothy. He once called Timothy his 'beloved 'child', but now Paul longs for the younger man's support and understanding: 'Do your best to come before winter.' I hope he made it.

■ PRAYER
God, thank you that you are with us in times of need – and thank you that so too are our 'brothers and sisters' in the fellowship of faith. Amen

The Gift of Years

 Debbie Thrower founded and leads The Gift of Years programme. She has pioneered the Anna Chaplaincy model, offering spiritual care to older people, and is widely involved in training and advocacy. Visit **thegiftofyears.org.uk** to find out more.

Debbie writes…

I was struck lately by three conversations I've had with people in the second half of life. Each has a bearing on the themes of this issue.

One widow who'd moved into a care home spoke about her marriage: 'Some couples face out, their lives full of connections,' she said. 'But we faced in.' Lamenting the loss of her husband three years earlier, she described how they'd had to lean on each other during some very challenging years with their son with behavioural problems.

Another man in his 80s told me how difficult it was to come to terms with his wife's death because now there was a deep void in his life and he didn't know who he was anymore.

The third encounter was with a single woman who'd been her mother's carer for many years. They'd lived together, and her mother had died some months before: 'The hardest thing is that there is no one who loves me anymore.'

Questions of identity, the quality of our loving throughout a lifetime, who loves us now… These will occupy us in those quiet times when we are alone. May these reflections help you find meaning and purpose in the company of others – Christian writers – who've also walked this way.

Best wishes

Debbie

Meet Erica Roberts

Erica Roberts was born in Walsall but spent her formative years in Lincoln, where her father was a deputy headmaster before deciding to train for ordination. A former paediatric oncologist and palliative care specialist, Erica is now an Anglican priest herself and is passionate about her growing role as City Chaplain for Older People in Southampton. She has also recently founded a charity called 'Caraway: gathering the harvest in our older years'. She is married to Mark and they have three adult children, Harriet, Anna and Luke. Erica's sister is also an Anglican priest.

So, you were brought up in a Christian family?

Indeed. Very conventional, really: Sunday school, youth groups, holiday camps. And then in my latter teenage years, I started to have those huge apologetics questions and sadly I didn't receive any satisfactory answers at the time.

So I went off to university *not* diving into church, and over that time I wouldn't say I lost my faith, but it became less important to me. I married a non-Christian and we went out to Africa – to Ghana – not as missionaries but as doctors, and it was only really after the birth of our first child, Harriet, when we came back to England, that I came back to faith.

Did you always want to be a doctor?

No, I didn't. I don't see myself as a scientist; I'm inherently more interested in the humanities and languages. I am, however, a little bit stubborn. With both family and teachers assuming that I would take History and English at A Level, I responded by doing science and then of course the obvious vocational path is medicine.

Were you drawn to paediatrics right from the beginning?

As soon as I did my first clinical paediatrics placement – there was such joy and fun in the midst of illness. Children are very straightforward and as soon as they get better, they are back to normal. I loved the way they didn't hold those fears and anxieties as we tend to.

That doesn't mean to say it wasn't enormously challenging and, as a paediatric oncologist, some of the children with cancer would eventually die. But we got to know them and their families so well, and there was a real privilege in supporting them in those last phases of life. By that time I did have a faith again and I really think that was what sustained me.

How and when did the call to priesthood come?

Interesting story. When the children were aged eleven, five and two, we were on a family holiday in France when we were all in a nasty car accident, leaving me with a permanently damaged knee. I was in a French hospital for two to three weeks and then had six months off work while my knee and my badly broken leg healed – and I remember feeling incredibly vulnerable as I wrestled with those questions of identity: 'I can't be the person I've been made to be. I can't practise as a doctor. I can't be the wife I want to be. I can't be the mother I want to be. So who am I?' And it was as if everything was stripped away and the kernel that was left was the truth that I am a child of God. And although that was obvious and we all know it, there was that very profound moment of realisation that that was all that mattered. But I got better and went back to work, and the thought disappeared into the shadows.

So I had four years back at work. During that time, I had something like 17 more surgical interventions on my knee and over time it caused increasing problems. Yet I still felt very called to my work in paediatric oncology and I felt very strongly it was where God wanted me to be. But after the final surgery, I was out walking on my crutches and I just felt God say – I actually heard God speak, which doesn't happen very often – 'You don't need to do this anymore.' It wasn't 'You mustn't do it,' but 'You don't need to do it.' So I heard that, prayed, talked, reflected and then handed in my resignation.

Had you any thoughts of ordination at that point?

It had never even crossed my mind. I thought I just needed to rest and assumed I'd eventually go back into medicine, doing something a little bit different. But during that year I did a local theology course and absolutely fell in love with some of the nuances and debates in scripture and I decided to do an Open University theology degree.

About a year later, I was on retreat, reading Isaiah 55: 'Come to the waters... Nothing's impossible for me... I'm going to send you out...' and I just knew that God was calling me to ordination. So I phoned my friend: 'You're going to think I'm completely mad. I'm married to a non-Christian. There's nowhere near Southampton to train. But I think God's calling me to ordination.'

And there was silence at the other end of the phone – and you know what I'm going to say: it wasn't surprise or laughter, it was: 'At last!' And I was ordained in Winchester in 2010 and it's just been the most wonderful blessing.

How have you gone from paediatrics to a concern and love for working with older people?

In my Master's in Theology and Ministry, my dissertation was on 'The Theology of Personhood in Dementia'. I spent a whole wonderful year reflecting not just on dementia but on the inclusivity of the whole of God's people to God. Everyone has access to God, whoever we are, whatever our physical or cognitive ability, and I was just trying to work out what that means for the individual and those around the individual.

Having completed that, and obviously coming to the conclusion that someone living with dementia is not only known and loved and valued by God, but there is nowhere – as it says in Psalm 139 – that you can escape a knowing God, even if I can't understand how that happens. The person with dementia is always known by God, and being known by God means being understood in the past, the present and the future – that's true for all of us, whether we have dementia or not.

And you're very excited about a new charity you're developing?

Yes! It's called 'Caraway: gathering the harvest in our older years'. The name comes from Isaiah 28, which talks about caraway and cumin not being harvested by a threshing wheel or a cart, but by a stick and a rod. The idea is that these beautiful herbs that add spice to life can be harvested by anyone at any season of life, even if you're frail and vulnerable; we can still be resourceful in our older years. And Caraway will be in partnership with The Gift of Years, so we've already got three Anna Chaplains working under the umbrella of Caraway. It'll be about resourcing the local church to reach out into the community and care homes – all very exciting.

Sunrise, on May Morning

See that church tower? They used to sing from there
At dawn, each first of May,
Anthems of praise for the glory and power of creation,
And the cows in the fields turned their heads,
And the horses twitched their ears, and shook their manes,
And the hens clucked softly, and shifted on last night's eggs.
No longer. The choir's too old and few,
And the new rector's frightened of heights,
So there's no flag flown on even the greatest festivals.

But, as the sun rises on May Day, and the spring really starts,
The cows still turn their heads to listen,
And the horses still twitch their ears and shake out their manes,
And the hens still cluck, very softly, and shift on last night's eggs,
To hear the first shoots rustle from the soil,
As creation begins again.

Robert Ferguson (used with kind permission)
From *Late Starter* (AuthorHouse UK, 2018).

Late starter

 Robert Ferguson is one of those rare individuals who has moved out of a care home and back into independent living. Since losing his beloved wife Barbara, he has taken on a flat, got to grips with an iPhone, spent several days in Edinburgh conducting research for a novel and published his collected poems in a volume called *Late Starter* (AuthorHouse UK, 2018). He shares his story:

I was brought up by non-religious parents in Peterborough. Despite enjoying many other gifts from being a cathedral chorister and being educated at the cathedral grammar school, by my early 20s I was a confirmed scientific rationalist.

In time, grace was provided through my wife, Barbara, and her vicar. A devoted Anglo-Catholic, Barbara's teasing, 'If there's nothing in it, it won't hurt you,' eventually drew me to her church, and her ex-Eighth-Army vicar immediately made me an altar server. At last I learned, through practice, what God and worship were all about.

Ten years later, encouraged by several inspiring teachers, I was trained and licensed as a Lay Reader in a pretty group of parishes in rural Kent. Again, practice stimulated learning, and my faith deepened.

Twenty years after that, now in the Midlands, I collapsed and was medically retired. Slowly recovering, my then-vicar took me off for my first monastic retreat. For ten years, immersion in the 'Offices and Mass' culture of various monasteries sustained daily duties at home as sacristan in our little parish church, and the writing of articles, booklets and 'soul-poems' for our parish magazine. I found particular inspiration in the example of St Francis of Assisi, and became a Companion of the Society of St Francis.

Then cancer struck both my wife and me. No longer capable of looking after ourselves, we moved into a care home. More grace, along with exemplary medical treatment, allowed us to institute a weekly Sunday worship service there and to lead a residents' poetry group. But when my dear Barbara died, six years later, I was able to move out of the care home to resume life in a parish community and to rebuild a support network of friends old and new.

To this end, I sought out writers' groups, joined two, and was made wonderfully welcome. Through them, I learned quickly, made mistakes and contacts, and found what perhaps I should have done all my life. Now in my 70s, I am discovering the joy and comfort of service in support of the following generations, in a church with doors large enough to allow the entry – and, on a good day, the exit – of my mobility scooter.

I remain convinced that the social functions of the church must derive from, and therefore be a most important second to, the worship of God, and that example, teaching and work are the keys to faith and to the retention of the faithful. I am also confident that, within the church, there is a place for everyone and that, when this life ends, God will welcome us all with the love and correction of a true Father in heaven.

Everybody needs a rock

Anne Townsend

When my eldest grandchild was four years old, she and her family lived by a little lake on the edge of a beautiful pine forest on the outskirts of Seattle. When I visited from England, I would often be tasked with taking her for as long an afternoon walk as I could manage, while her baby brother was being bathed and fed.

She had a children's book called *Everybody Needs a Rock*. In America, they often use the word 'rock' for those hard little objects that we call 'stones'. On our walks, we'd while away the hours hunting for rocks and grading them according to how special they were to us.

Two of my favourites were treasures we'd discovered on the beach at Puget Sound – one was a beautiful rounded grey stone half covered in barnacles, and the other, its non-identical twin, glistened pure white in the sunshine. They sit on a shelf in my home 20 years later, bursting with never-to-be-forgotten memories.

When it was my turn to read her bedtime story and say her prayers, we'd sometimes each grasp our favourite 'rock' tightly in cupped hands, enjoy it and talk about some of the ways in which God is there as an indestructible solid rock for us.

We enjoyed those times so much that I'm going to share how some of our discoveries have developed and blossomed in my mind over the years.

1 Peter 2:5 (NIV)

Animal, vegetable, mineral?

You also, like living stones, are being built into a spiritual house to be a holy priesthood, offering spiritual sacrifices acceptable to God through Jesus Christ.

I have memories of seemingly endless childhood car journeys when we'd play 'Animal, vegetable or mineral?'. Anything 'mineral', like a stone, could not by definition be living.

The Bible abounds in metaphors – such as 'living stones' – which declare that one thing is another. These words are not literally true but, in context, communicate a concept that is closer to the truth.

The word 'living' in Greek is *zoe* – a small word with a big meaning. It's about something greater than mere human existence. It's about fullness of life – God's uncreated, eternal life that we have the capacity to experience. When we tune in to this, we become 'living' – *zoe* – 'stones'.

It's often said that you need to be young and fit to survive ageing. Managing life's smallest tasks becomes painfully tricky with arthritis; travelling becomes a major undertaking when vision is reduced; and storytelling involves mental gymnastics if the correct words refuse to present themselves. Yet, Jesus tells us, 'I have come that they may have life, and have it to the full' (John 10:10).

God's promised 'abundant life' is not just for the young and strong; it is still plenteously available as we grow older.

■ PRAYER

Living God, enlarge my capacity to tune in to, and draw on, your abundant life. Help me to remember it's still always available. Amen

Psalm 78:15–16 (NIV)

Ration books redundant

He split the rocks in the wilderness and gave them water as abundant as the seas; he brought streams out of a rocky crag and made water flow down like rivers.

As missionaries, my family and I understood water shortage. Our family of five was permitted just six cans of water daily. Visiting a large Bangkok hotel, my five-year-old daughter expressed her dismay at the top of her voice, 'Mummy, why is all this beautiful water being wasted in the toilet?'

Psalm 78 speaks of times when God, or his messenger, literally struck rock and water gushed out. God promises that when life feels as hard as rock, he will transform even our worst scenarios, making them not just bearable but precious.

My mother lived to be 102 years old. I was amazed at her capacity to find joy in limited situations. 'When it's dark, I don't always remember whether it's day or night,' she'd explain, 'So I phone the operator and she even tells me the day and the date as well – I'm so blessed.' Unable to master washing machines, she would stand under her shower, fully dressed, rubbing soap over her clothes. 'They smell gorgeous,' she'd say, 'And dry quickly on these wonderful radiators.'

My mother accepted her outer world – restricted by pain, arthritis, widowhood and care-home life – and when it came to her internal world, God generously supplied the water of life in rocky situations.

■ PRAYER

Abundant God, may I recognise your generosity despite my limitations, and may I be generous with others. Amen

1 Peter 2:5; Ephesians 2:10a (NIV)

Finishing touches

You also, like living stones, are being built into a spiritual house to be a holy priesthood, offering spiritual sacrifices acceptable to God through Jesus Christ… For we are God's handiwork, created in Christ Jesus to do good works.

As we read in an earlier reflection by Erica Roberts, the sculptor Michelangelo never saw a chunk of rock as a formless, inanimate object. He studied it and gradually unlocked its secrets, visualising the living figure encased within the stone and straining to break free. In his words, 'The sculpture is already complete within the marble block… I just have to chisel away the superfluous material.' For me, his most moving sculptures are four unfinished works depicting slaves – not totally freed from their stony prisons.

As we have seen, the Bible calls us God's 'living stones'. We are also called God's 'handiwork', 'workmanship' and 'artwork'. According to the Greek work used – *poiema* – each of us is God's poem. Psychologists suggest that in life's later stages, we often complete some unfinished business. We mentally revisit old traumas, finally making sense of them and finding peace. We ponder skewed relationships and attempt to straighten them. Above all, we are given fresh opportunity to allow God to put the finishing touches to the person – the 'poem' – we really are.

Picasso comments, 'Art is never finished, only abandoned.' God never abandons us and hasn't finished shaping us yet.

■ **PRAYER**

Creating God, I'm here longing for you to transform me into the person I really am. Amen

Psalm 31:2 (NIV)

Emergency service

Turn your ear to me, come quickly to my rescue; be my rock of refuge, a strong fortress to save me.

We were exploring the back of beyond in an isolated area in Thailand. My children enjoyed letting off steam at the foot of a mountain. Then, suddenly, the sky blackened and within milliseconds deluging monsoon rain drenched us. I knew what to do. My friend had told me of a hidden cave and we fled there for shelter. We were safe until the rain stopped and we could sunbathe again.

The Hebrew word *tsur*, translated as 'rock' in this psalm, is frequently used to symbolise God. God is available as an emergency 'rock of refuge'. We can dive into the Almighty's sheltering cave whenever life's monsoons threaten our stability.

Ageing renders us more vulnerable than before. Change may throw us. We're expected to pay fares with cards not coins, and to sing hymns from screens not books. Managing the television remote becomes a challenge and, much more seriously, advances in medicine may mean we're asked difficult questions about treatments and interventions – for ourselves or our loved ones.

But in all situations and emergencies, major and minor, God is available with a swift rescuing response. God offers a rock where we can safely hide until our inner storms settle and we can face the world again.

■ **PRAYER**

My rescuer, rock, refuge and fortress – may I always remember you are there for me. Amen

1 Peter 2:4–6 (NIV)

Cornering securely

As you come to him, the living stone – rejected by humans but chosen by God and precious to him – you also, like living stones, are being built into a spiritual house to be a holy priesthood, offering spiritual sacrifices acceptable to God through Jesus Christ. For in scripture it says: 'See, I lay a stone in Zion, a chosen and precious cornerstone, and the one who trusts in him will never be put to shame.'

Prefabricated houses fire today's imaginations. Take a giant Lego kit, fit the pieces together, add drains, water and electrics, and – 'Hey presto!' – there's a new home.

Construction work in the Bible was totally different. Once the foundations were laid, a large cornerstone was carefully positioned to unite two main walls. It was strong enough to carry everything built on it. It was shaped from expensive rock so that it would look beautiful and never cave in.

In the temple in Jerusalem, according to one estimate, the cornerstones were 20–30 feet long, weighed over 100 tons and were extraordinarily strong.

Jesus is the cornerstone of our faith. As we mull over this thought today, we may find ourselves relaxing and resting in the total security that is ours in God. Getting older has its moments. We sometimes wobble. We may sometimes be afraid of the future. But our God – our cornerstone – doesn't change and is solidly dependable and immovable, no matter what.

■ **PRAYER**

God, my cornerstone, please help me to relax in your dependability. Amen

Psalm 71:3 (NIV)

Safer than safe

Be my rock of refuge, to which I can always go; give the command to save me, for you are my rock and my fortress.

A fortress built on rock, like Edinburgh Castle, offers safe, solid protection, but I'm hardly likely to run there for help. My dictionary adds that a fortress also refers to 'a person… not susceptible to outside influence or disturbance'. That resonates with me. I'd run to someone like that for help.

Even after all these years, I remember how my Latin teacher often changed her mind according to the opinions of others or what would please the headmistress. My French teacher, by contrast, was rock solid, consistent and reliable. We knew exactly where we were with her and felt safe, and because of that we were happy to do what she said and obey her instructions.

We have a God who is rock solid and consistent. God doesn't change with every swing of the weathercock, or with fashion or opinion. His love and care for us never wavers and he is our fortress forever.

■ **PRAYER**

Rock-solid God, remind me today that I can always trust in you and in the security of your unchanging love. Amen

1 Peter 2:6 (NIV)

Most precious stone

'See, I lay a stone in Zion, a chosen and precious cornerstone, and the one who trusts in him will never be put to shame.'

This is such a rich verse from 1 Peter that I make no apology for quoting it again. As a teenager, the renowned 19th-century Baptist leader Charles Spurgeon found his wings as a preacher during a cottage service when no adult was available to preach. He focused on this verse, and in particular the words 'This stone is precious,' explaining later: 'I was in the first flush of youthful love and couldn't be silent when my precious Jesus was the subject.'

Afterwards, the villagers were curious: 'How old are you?' 'Under 60,' he fudged. 'Yes, and under 16!' an old lady countered. 'Forget my age, just think of Jesus and his preciousness,' Charles urged, and promised to return.

Sharing Jesus' value comes more readily to some than to others. As we age, we might still be able to lead meetings and services, and to preach. Most of us can still pray for other people. Some offer the invaluable gift of time, and sit silently listening when appropriate. Others 'chat Jesus' in the supermarket or the bus queue.

In words from an Agape Communion, 'We remember that Jesus comes to us in the local and distant stranger, in the hungry, in those we find unlovely, in the thirsty, in those who most annoy us, in the homeless and in those needing us to warm them.'

■ PRAYER

Jesus, you are of supreme value. May I share you generously. Amen

Matthew 16:16–18a (NIV)

Name games

Simon Peter answered, 'You are the Messiah, the Son of the living God.' Jesus replied, 'Blessed are you, Simon son of Jonah, for this was not revealed to you by flesh and blood, but by my Father in heaven. And I tell you that you are Peter, and on this rock I will build my church.'

My family loves nicknames. I became 'Moomintrol', from a children's book. Eventually, this was abbreviated to 'Min' and, when grand-children arrived, to 'Grandmin'.

Jesus playfully uses a double meaning in talking about Peter's blessing. Jesus starts off calling him Jonah's son, Simon. Then he pays him the highest compliment by renaming him Peter – 'Petros' – a solid rock. And then the Greek word imperceptibly slides into the feminine 'Petra'. One interpretation is that 'Petra' refers to Jesus himself – the enduring cornerstone on which the church is founded.

Theologian Tom Wright suggests: 'If Peter was prepared to say that Jesus was the Messiah, then Jesus was prepared to say that, with this allegiance, Peter would himself be the foundation for his new building.'*

Each of us plays a unique part in God's work of building his church. We are the raw building materials – bricks, stones, wood, mortar – from which he constructs this community. Ageism doesn't exist here. When we are in exactly the right place, our contribution to the whole is essential and our true value becomes apparent.

■ **PRAYER**

God of construction, place me exactly where I'll best fit as you build your church. Amen

*Tom Wright, *Matthew for Everyone: Part 2* (SPCK, 2002), p. 8.

Genesis 28:18–22 (NIV, abridged)

Cradle of rock

Early the next morning Jacob took the stone he had placed under his head and set it up as a pillar and poured oil on top of it. He called that place Bethel… Then Jacob made a vow, saying, 'If God will be with me and will watch over me on this journey I am taking and will give me food to eat and clothes to wear so that I return safely to my father's household, then the Lord will be my God and this stone that I have set up as a pillar will be God's house.'

I have a basket filled with assorted little stones given as mementos. One is special. Silently holding it, I try to drift into my inner space. Cradling it in my cupped hand, I remember that my name is carved on the palm of God's hand and that I'm cradled in God's arms. My God-stone is solid and indestructible. At such moments, I glimpse the meaning at the heart of worship.

The first biblical use of a rock in worship was when Jacob took his stony pillow, poured oil on it and promised to follow God, provided God played his part in looking after Jacob.

Our situation is different: we live in the world transformed forever by the coming of Jesus. We know – though we sometimes forget – that we don't have to make bargains with God. His love and care are without condition for those who love his Son. Holding my 'God-stone', I'm reminded of this certainty.

■ **PRAYER**
Cradling God, may we rest in your arms. Amen

Psalm 19:14 (NIV)

Rock bottom

May these words of my mouth and this meditation of my heart be pleasing in your sight, Lord, my Rock and my Redeemer.

C.S. Lewis describes Psalm 19 as 'the greatest poem in the psalter and one of the greatest lyrics in the world'.

As a child in church, every Sunday I used to hear the preacher – often my own father – repeat verse 14 at the beginning of every sermon. It grew so familiar to me that the words became a sort of mantra – they washed over me and I lost their meaning.

But these words are not intended only to serve as the introduction to sermons, or to signal to a congregation that it's time to sit down. We can use them every day when we come before God in the quiet of our own room. If we have enough courage to really mean what we're saying when we use them, we'll be inviting God to scrutinise both our utterances and every thought and emotion buried deep in our heart of hearts – at the bedrock of our being. We may feel embarrassed and even ashamed, but we will discover how deeply God loves us.

The God who knows our depths is the God who redeems and transforms us.

■ PRAYER

May these words of my mouth and this meditation of my heart be pleasing in your sight, Lord, my Rock and my Redeemer. Amen

Being useful

David Butterfield

Can you think of an occasion when someone expressed thanks to you for something you had done? How did you feel in that moment? I imagine your spirits were lifted because you felt you had been useful and that this had been appreciated.

The apostle Paul's shortest letter was written to a man called Philemon, whose slave Onesimus had run away. Onesimus happened to meet Paul and he became a Christian. While Paul was in prison, Onesimus was really useful to him and his ministry. Sometime later, Paul decided he should send Onesimus back to Philemon and he wrote him a very moving letter in which he says, 'Welcome him as you would welcome me.'

The name Onesimus means 'useful' and in his letter Paul tells Philemon that, whereas in the past Onesimus had been 'useless' to him, now he would be 'useful'.

When we are retired and growing older, it is easy to feel that we are of little or no use compared with earlier times in our lives. However, this need not be so. In this series of reflections, we will explore how we can be an 'Onesimus' to God and to others by being useful to them.

Mark 1:9–11 (NIV, abridged)

Being a child of God

Jesus… was baptised by John in the Jordan. Just as Jesus was coming up out of the water, he saw heaven being torn open and the Spirit descending on him like a dove. And a voice came from heaven: 'You are my Son, whom I love; with you I am well pleased.'

Why did God tell Jesus that he was pleased with him? What had he done to deserve such an affirmation? The answer is that Jesus had not done anything – he was yet to begin his ministry. He began his work knowing that he was loved by his Father because of who he was – his Son – not because of anything he had done.

When we think about being useful to God, it is important that this stems from a deep sense of being loved and accepted by God as we are. Yet there's something within us that seeks to win God's acceptance and love through what we do.

Spend a moment now, and each time you come to one of these reflections, imagining your heavenly Father speaking these words to you: 'You are my child, whom I love; with you I am well pleased.' Remind yourself that God loves you because he is love, not because of what you do.

When we have this deep assurance, we will be ready, as Jesus was, to serve him with a renewed sense of confidence and worth.

■ **PRAYER**
Heavenly Father, help me to know, deep within my spirit, that you love me just as I am. Amen

Romans 12:6–8 (NIV)

Gifted by God

We have different gifts, according to the grace given to each of us. If your gift is prophesying, then prophesy in accordance with your faith; if it is serving, then serve; if it is teaching, then teach; if it is to encourage, then give encouragement; if it is giving, then give generously; if it is to lead, do it diligently; if it is to show mercy, do it cheerfully.

In my retirement, I have tried to learn to cook. I've had four goes at making a crème caramel from a recipe by Delia Smith. Unfortunately, only one of these attempts was completely successful. I think playing a church organ is far, far easier.

Of all the tasks we do, some seem really hard, whereas others flow naturally. This can be because in some areas we have a God-given gift. That's why for me playing a church organ is a joy, but cooking is hard work.

Paul tells us that we all have different gifts and it's important to discern which ones God may have given to us. In different phases of life these might change, and it's good to reassess them prayerfully over time because God might want to gift us in new ways.

When we use our gifts for the benefit of others, we will be useful to them and be a blessing to them.

■ PRAYER

Heavenly Father, please show me one area in which you have gifted me. Help me to use this gift to bless someone this coming week. Amen

1 Peter 5:12 (GNB)

Write a letter today

I write you this brief letter with the help of Silas, whom I regard as a faithful Christian. I want to encourage you and give my testimony that this is the true grace of God. Stand firm in it.

My wife Irene and I have both kept the letters we wrote to each other before we were married. I can recall how important her letters were to me. I was encouraged by what she wrote and by how she signed off with love and kisses.

In his second letter, Peter tells his readers that he is writing because he wants to encourage them. If we want to say something positive to someone, it can be better to write it rather than say it, because the person receiving it can read it again and again and the encouragement endures.

As you look back, can you think of someone who has been a significant help and a support to you in your Christian journey, whether some time ago or more recently? You could write a short letter saying how much you appreciate the encouragement you received or, if that's difficult, perhaps you could dictate it to a friend or a carer. By doing this, you will build this person up in the faith, and because it is written it will be a lasting encouragement.

■ **PRAYER**
Heavenly Father, may your Holy Spirit bring to my mind someone to whom I could write a letter of encouragement today. Amen

Colossians 4:2-3 (NIV)

Focusing our prayers

Devote yourselves to prayer, being watchful and thankful. And pray for us, too, that God may open a door for our message, so that we may proclaim the mystery of Christ, for which I am in chains.

I retired at 65 after serving as an ordained minister in the Church of England for 40 years. During the final phase of my ministry, I had oversight of clergy and churches. As I travelled a great deal, I didn't have a church base and missed the support of a local congregation. So I decided to send a prayer diary each month to some trusted friends and family. I very much valued the support of those who prayed for me during those years.

When Paul wrote to the Christians in Colossae, he asked them to pray for him. Even when we are limited physically because of age or infirmity, we can still pray. I find it really helps if I can be specific in my prayers rather than general.

Among the many Christian organisations that ask for our support, we could choose just one to pray for in a focused way using its prayer diary. Or perhaps we know someone in Christian ministry who could feature regularly in our prayers.

■ PRAYER

Heavenly Father, may my prayers for others make a positive difference to their lives and ministries. Amen

Psalm 25:16–17 (NRSV)

An answer to prayer

Turn to me and be gracious to me, for I am lonely and afflicted.
Relieve the troubles of my heart, and bring me out of my distress.

In October 2017, a former surgeon was in the news for expressing his concerns about loneliness, which he said was becoming an epidemic. He said that rates of loneliness had doubled since the 1980s.

King David knew what it felt like to be lonely. In Psalm 25, we hear him crying out to God about it. We don't know how God responded to David's prayer. For him, the cause of it was the threat posed by his enemies, but loneliness can come upon us for a variety of reasons, and at any age.

There may be many people today who, like David, cry out to God in their loneliness. I wonder how God might answer their prayer. Could we be the answer to someone's prayer?

We could ask God to bring someone to mind who may be lonely and then pick up the telephone for a chat, or even visit that person. This is something the apostle James encouraged his readers to do ('visit orphans and widows in their affliction', James 1:27, RSV) but even if it's not possible to visit, we can still pray for them in their loneliness.

By doing these things, we'll not only be useful to God and to someone who is feeling lonely, but we'll also feel blessed ourselves if we are feeling lonely too.

■ **PRAYER**

Heavenly Father, please be gracious to all those who are lonely and bring them out of their distress. Amen

Luke 6:38 (NRSV)

A cheerful giver

'Give, and it will be given to you. A good measure, pressed down, shaken together, running over, will be put into your lap; for the measure you give will be the measure you get back.'

When our son Jon was ten, our church had a harvest appeal for Tearfund. He was saving up to buy a Lego Western Gold Mine, but decided to give £5 from his savings to Tearfund. Two days later, I went to see my elderly father who, a couple of weeks earlier, had forgotten Jon's birthday. Without prompting, he said, 'I forgot Jon's birthday – here's £10.' So Jon learned early on the truth of Jesus' words, 'Give, and it will be given to you.'

There are many places in the scriptures where we are encouraged to be generous. In the account of the widow's mite, Jesus taught that generosity is measured by what is left over after we have given our gift. We can be useful to God and other people by being generous to a favourite charity or some other worthy cause according to our means. We could leave a legacy, which would make a lasting difference that will outlive us.

Perhaps it's because we can be fearful of being generous that Jesus assures us that when we seek first his kingdom and his righteousness, 'all these things will be given to you as well' (Matthew 6:33, NIV).

■ **PRAYER**

Heavenly Father, thank you for your generosity to me. Help me to reflect your generosity and be a blessing to others. Amen

Acts 4:36–37 (NIV)

Encourage one another

Joseph, a Levite from Cyprus, whom the apostles called Barnabas (which means 'son of encouragement'), sold a field he owned and brought the money and put it at the apostles' feet.

Were you ever given a nickname when you were at school? If so, was it unkind or was it friendly? With a surname like Butterfield, you may be able to imagine that the nicknames I was given were not all complimentary.

In these verses from Acts, we are told how a man called Joseph was given a nickname by the apostles. They called him Barnabas, which means 'Encourager'. What a delightful man he must have been, and his nickname must have been a wonderful affirmation for him.

Sometimes we say helpful, affirming things to people without realising it. However, I think we can go one better than that by deliberately thinking about how we can say something encouraging to those we encounter, whether we know them well or not.

In our times of prayer, we could ask God to put into our minds an appreciative nickname for someone we know. To offer such a word of encouragement could change that person's day; it might even be remembered for years to come.

■ PRAYER

Heavenly Father, please give me an opportunity to affirm someone today. Amen

Psalm 149:4 (NKJV)

Taking the humbler part

For the Lord takes pleasure in His people; He will beautify the humble with salvation.

Can you remember a time when life was much busier than it is today? You may have had responsibility for a number of very significant things: running a home, bringing up a family or dealing with the pressures of a demanding job. At times, your more important tasks would slip down your to-do list because of the many small, urgent matters that needed to be attended to. Had someone offered to do one of those more menial tasks, it would have made life so much easier for you.

In contrast, in later life you may find that you have plenty of time. Since I retired, I have certainly found this to be so. Might it be possible for us to offer to do a menial task for someone who is extremely busy? In a verse of the hymn, 'Come down, O love divine',* there is a touching reference to the 'true lowliness of heart, which takes the humbler part'.

It could be something as simple as making a phone call, baking a cake, tidying a sock drawer, wrapping presents or posting a letter for someone, or it could be asking them if there is some aspect of their busy, stressful life you could pray for. By taking 'the humbler part', we might find that we are really useful to someone who is living a hectic life.

■ **PRAYER**

Heavenly Father, please show me how I might be able to play a humble part in someone's life and be a blessing to that person. Amen

*Bianco de Siena (1367–1434)

Hebrews 13:2 (NIV)

Love your neighbour

Do not forget to show hospitality to strangers, for by so doing some people have shown hospitality to angels without knowing it.

When my wife and I moved into our house not so long ago, we met a few of our new neighbours in the first few weeks. As Christmas approached, we decided to invite them round for mince pies and mulled wine one Sunday afternoon. A week before, as we rang our neighbours' doorbells to invite them, I confess that I felt slightly nervous.

However, I needn't have worried because there was a positive response. One person said how good it was to gather together as neighbours. It was a very simple thing to do and we intend to do it again.

Our situations will all be very different. If we live in a care home, we may only be able to invite someone to join us for a cup of tea in our room. Others may be able to invite people to their home for a full-blown meal. Yet whatever form it takes, offering hospitality in this way helps to build a sense of community and builds relationships. It's also a lovely – and very biblical – way of showing God's love.

■ PRAYER

Heavenly Father, I pray for your blessing on those who live near to me. Please show me how I might extend a hand of friendship and hospitality to one or more of them. Amen

Proverbs 15:23b (NRSV)

The power of words

A word in season, how good it is!

In 2017, I had to undergo an invasive medical test. You can imagine my relief when afterwards I was told that nothing sinister was revealed. I was struck by how the medical staff went out of their way to put me at ease and to make sure that I was okay throughout the whole procedure.

As I reflected on this later, I decided to write a letter to the hospital expressing how impressed I was by the quality of care I had received and to sing the praises of the UK National Health Service. I soon received a warm reply from the doctor concerned – people usually only wrote if they had a complaint. Amidst their busy and stressful work, I hope that my words made a positive difference by encouraging the staff, and that in some small way, in taking time to write my letter, I was helpful to them as they had been to me.

In our everyday lives, we receive help from many people. It might be a heating engineer, a carer, a neighbour or a health visitor. If we were to express a word of appreciation to them by sending a card, or by a carefully chosen spoken word, it could make a real difference to how they feel as they go about their work.

Through these ten reflections, we have been focusing on how we can each be an 'Onesimus' to those around us by being useful to them as Onesimus was to the apostle Paul. May his example continue to inspire us.

■ PRAYER

Heavenly Father, help me to bless those around me by being an 'Onesimus' to them. Amen

Let's build a better world through gifts in wills

Today's children are global citizens. Modern technology means that the latest news from across the world can be broadcast in seconds, and communications with North or South America, Africa, Asia or Australasia are simply a click away.

As travel between countries becomes faster, we also tend to move around more. Many of today's children will live alongside people from other countries with different cultures, customs and beliefs. Even within Christianity itself, there can be differences in how the faith is celebrated from one country to the next.

Our Barnabas in Schools team has been exploring this theme all year with schools across England and Wales. Through 'Christianity around the World', they've taken children on a journey to learn about how faith is practised in countries such as Ethiopia, Argentina, Spain and Russia. It's all part of our aim to help the next generation grow to love and accept each other and ultimately build a better world.

You can be part of this vision too by leaving a gift in your will to BRF. Gifts in wills help us teach Christianity creatively within the school curriculum, and every year over 20,000 children experience our Barnabas RE Days exploring 'Christianity around the World' and other themes.

Gifts in wills don't need to be huge to help us make a real difference and, for every £1 we receive, we typically invest 95p back into charitable activities.

For further information about making a gift to BRF
in your will, please visit **brf.org.uk/lastingdifference**,
contact **+44 (0)1865 319700** or email **giving@brf.org.uk**.

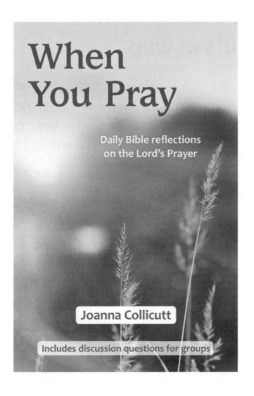

In this updated edition of a classic text, Joanna Collicutt shows how growing as a Christian is rooted in the prayer Jesus gave us. As we pray the Lord's Prayer, we express our relationship with God, absorb gospel values and are also motivated to live them out. As we pray to the Father, in union with the Son, through the power of the Spirit, so we begin to take on the character of Christ.

When You Pray
Daily Bible reflections on the Lord's Prayer
Joanna Collicutt
978 0 85746 867 3   £8.99
brfonline.org.uk

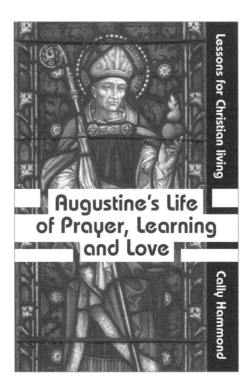

This book makes the great saint accessible, charting Augustine's beginnings of faith, struggles with doubt, fear of scorn and mockery, worries about whether he is 'good enough', through public affirmation and church membership, into a dedicated life of worship, Bible reading, thinking about faith and living it. It concludes with moments of prayer from Augustine's life, in which he glimpses visions of God, encouraging the reader to take their own next steps in discipleship.

Augustine's Life of Prayer, Learning and Love
Lessons for Christian living
Cally Hammond
978 0 85746 714 0 £9.99
brfonline.org.uk

To order

Online: **brfonline.org.uk**
Telephone: +44 (0)1865 319700
Mon–Fri 9.15–17.30
Post: complete this form and send to the address below

Delivery times within the UK are normally 15 working days. Prices are correct at the time of going to press but may change without prior notice.

Title	Issue*	Price	Qty	Total
When You Pray		£8.99		
Augustine's Life of Prayer, Learning and Love		£9.99		
Bible Reflections for Older People (single copy)	Sep 19/Jan 20*	£5.05		

delete as appropriate

POSTAGE AND PACKING CHARGES			
Order value	UK	Europe	Rest of world
Under £7.00	£2.00	£5.00	£7.00
£7.00–£29.99	£3.00	£9.00	£15.00
£30.00 and over	FREE	£9.00 + 15% of order value	£15.00 + 20% of order value

Total value of books	
Postage and packing	
Total for this order	

Please complete in BLOCK CAPITALS

Title .... First name/initials .... Surname...

Address ....

.... Postcode ....

Acc. No. .... Telephone ....

Email ....

Method of payment

❑ Cheque (made payable to BRF)   ❑ MasterCard / Visa

Card no. [ ][ ][ ][ ] [ ][ ][ ][ ] [ ][ ][ ][ ] [ ][ ][ ][ ]

Expires end [M][M] [Y][Y]   Security code* [ ][ ][ ]   Last 3 digits on the reverse of the card

Signature* .... Date .... /............ /............
*ESSENTIAL IN ORDER TO PROCESS YOUR ORDER

Please return this form to:

BRF, 15 The Chambers, Vineyard, Abingdon OX14 3FE | enquiries@brf.org.uk
To read our terms and conditions, please visit **brfonline.org.uk/terms**.

BIBLE REFLECTIONS FOR OLDER PEOPLE GROUP SUBSCRIPTION FORM

> All our Bible reading notes can be ordered online
> by visiting **biblereadingnotes.org.uk/subscriptions**

The group subscription rate for *Bible Reflections for Older People* will be £15.15 per person until April 2020.

☐ I would like to take out a group subscription for .... (*quantity*) copies.

☐ Please start my order with the September 2019 / January 2020 / May 2020* issue.
I would like to pay annually/receive an invoice with each edition of the notes.* (*delete as appropriate*)

Please do not send any money with your order. Send your order to BRF and we will send you an invoice. The group subscription year is from 1 May to 30 April. If you start subscribing in the middle of a subscription year we will invoice you for the remaining number of issues left in that year.

Name and address of the person organising the group subscription:

Title .... First name/initials .... Surname...

Address...

....Postcode ....

Telephone .... Email...

Church...

Name of minister ....

Name and address of the person paying the invoice if the invoice needs to be sent directly to them:

Title .... First name/initials .... Surname...

Address...

....Postcode ....

Telephone .... Email...

Please return this form to:
BRF, 15 The Chambers, Vineyard, Abingdon OX14 3FE | enquiries@brf.org.uk
To read our terms and conditions, please visit **brfonline.org.uk/terms**.

The Bible Reading Fellowship is a Registered Charity (233280)

BIBLE REFLECTIONS FOR OLDER PEOPLE INDIVIDUAL/GIFT SUBSCRIPTION FORM

> To order online, please visit **biblereadingnotes.org.uk/subscriptions**

☐ I would like to take out a subscription (*complete your name and address details only once*)
☐ I would like to give a gift subscription (*please provide both names and addresses*)

Title .... First name/initials .... Surname...

Address...

.... Postcode ....

Telephone.............................Email...

Gift subscription name ....

Gift subscription address ....

.... Postcode.................................

Gift message (*20 words max. or include your own gift card*):

Please send *Bible Reflections for Older People* beginning with the September 2019 / January 2020 / May 2020* issue (*delete as appropriate):

(*please tick box*) | **UK** | **Europe** | **Rest of world**

Bible Reflections for Older People ☐ £19.20 ☐ £27.00 ☐ £31.05

Total enclosed £ .... (*cheques should be made payable to 'BRF'*)

Please charge my MasterCard / Visa ☐ Debit card ☐ with £ ....

Card no. ☐☐☐☐ ☐☐☐☐ ☐☐☐☐ ☐☐☐☐

Expires end ☐☐ ☐☐ Security code* ☐☐☐ Last 3 digits on the reverse of the card

Signature* .... Date ..../......./.......
*ESSENTIAL IN ORDER TO PROCESS YOUR ORDER

Please return this form to:
BRF, 15 The Chambers, Vineyard, Abingdon OX14 3FE | enquiries@brf.org.uk
To read our terms and conditions, please visit **brfonline.org.uk/terms**.

The Bible Reading Fellowship is a Registered Charity (233280)